The
Retirement
ENDGAME

How to Cash in Your Chips at the Wall Street Casino & Retire with Peace of Mind

Jerry Whitmire

Founder, JW Financial Consulting, LLC

Acknowledgements

I want to dedicate this book to my parents, JERRY AND PATTY WHITMIRE. You have both been great examples of what parents should be. If I can become half the person that you two have shown me, I will be OK in this life. You both have pushed me to be successful and have always been there for encouragement. The life lessons and hard work that I witnessed in you both has definitely played a big factor in my success in life and business. The way you raised me has enabled me to do the right thing for so many families over the last 11 years. You instilled in me a deep warmth and compassion that motivates me to properly guide my clients as their advisor with the highest integrity. You both said I should write a book and share my process with the world. This is **THE BOOK**, and I appreciate you more than you will ever know!

The creativity and vision for a book like this doesn't just happen. It is born out of a lifetime of events and wonderful people who have come across my path.

FRANK LOZANO: I have worked with a lot of people throughout my career that have embraced my work ethic, offered to help my career, yet try to impose their marketing systems. You, my friend, have embraced my fast pace and hunger to keep the "Jerry process" alive and moving forward. We've had a good run --- this is only the beginning. Thanks!

DILLON HAMMON - Thanks you so much for taking my words, thoughts, and creative juices to the next level in assisting me to write this book. You are a real professional, and I would recommend you to anyone wanting to take their experiences and put it to paper.

NOLAN HAMMON – Thank you for helping me create a marketing brand with *"The Retirement Endgame"*. Your graphic design magic in creating my website and marketing process to coincide with your brother's writing has been truly enjoyable.

Preface

Something's happening here…. What it is ain't exactly clear!

Stephen Stills – *For What it's Worth*

What the Hell is going on with Wall Street?

Is it just me or is there something going on for the last 15 years on Wall Street that just doesn't make sense?

I mean ---- come on folks! We experienced two 50% drops in the stock market over the last 15 years.

I know, I know. Things are just peachy now that the stock markets have had a record rebound since the disastrous economic tsunami that saw 75% of Wall Street implode.

You know: the guys who were telling you to stay the course in 2001 and 2008.

Coincidentally the only firms that survived did so on your dime through Government bailouts!

Who bailed those out who couldn't retire when their retirement plans were downsized, along with most of their jobs?

Let's go back to the not too distant past--- say May of 2009 when the stock market was at it's devastating low--- when Jim Cramer and other TV financial pundits where near hysterical in

1

their appeals to the President to allow Congress to bail all the risk takers out because of their **GREED.**

Remember May of 2009? Remember how you felt? Remember how scared you were that you'd never be able to retire because Wall Street had just scrambled your nest egg?

You're not holding this book right now because you're looking for the latest investment tip on how to double your current money in the next five years.

You're holding this book because you want to protect the money you can't afford to lose!

You know in your heart that this stock market recovery has been a carnival hawker's shell game: zero interest rates to the bankers who caused this mess in the first place, just so that they could hold unto it for over five years for billions of profit to themselves.

More jobs? No!

Relaxed lending environment to people and businesses that needed to create jobs and grow the economy? Seriously! Have you tried to qualify for a personal, real estate or business loan over past five years?

The Pit Bosses of the Casino

Well folks, here you are at the Wall Street Casino where fortunes are made and lost---- their fortunes, your losses!

Your largest liquid asset—your retirement plan--- is completely exposed once again to the whims of **FEAR and GREED.**

Your broker---- I mean, bookie---- tells you that the "betting sheets" (better known as the Research Reports) say it's all-good.

The stock market has doubled in six years after losing half your money twice in the prior nine, and you're told to stay in the Casino, have another drink and enjoy the free buffet!

Come on! Aren't you concerned about getting hammered again?

Can you afford to not call in your chips?

Aren't you just grateful that there was a recovery and you're OK if you don't lose it to the House again?

So why do you have that feeling that "Something's happening here--- What it is ain't exactly clear"?

What's happening here is that your financial future is a risk, and you're not clear what to do about it.

That is why you're holding this book in your hand!

You need advice you can trust. You need clarity in a smoke-filled casino. You need a lifetime solution to ensure your money won't run out before you do.

You need someone to encourage you to understand the meaning of **enough** --- and to help you put together a plan to safely protect and grow your money.

Your Retirement Plan needs *The RETIREMENT ENDGAME.*

That is why I wrote this book!

Contents

Chapter 1

Telling it the Way it is

Do you have money you can't afford to lose? Even if your only concern this week is whether to drive the Porsche or Benz, or which of your luxury houses to visit (all paid free and clear), then this book is probably still for you!

Maybe you need me to advise you to keep half your money in safe money strategies to ensure your financial peace of mind, and you and your Broker (Bookie) can play with the rest.

More than likely, unless you are silly-rich, you need to protect your money. Mike Tyson, Evander Holyfield and many professional athletes and entertainers made hundreds of millions of dollars in their careers.

Now they are **SILLY-BROKE!**

I don't care what age you are. If you have retirement savings at risk, and you can't afford to suffer another significant stock market correction, you should be concerned about protecting your financial future.

You owe it to yourself...... you owe it to your family!

If you aren't worried about having enough money to last through your retirement, you should be. Life is no Sunday at the beach --- it's hard. From our first day 'til our last we have to work for everything. We work hard for our families, relationships, and careers. You earned your way in this life. So why put yourself in a place where someone's stupid advice can take it from you.

Today the problem isn't just getting to retirement, but having plenty of time and money to enjoy it through retirement!

If we can beat both inflation and taxes when accumulating your retirement savings we have a shot at staying retired. I regularly have people come into my office or one of my seminars or workshops and they say: "We have a financial advisor who is recommending putting our life savings into a variable annuity or variable universal life policy, or the stock market. What do you recommend?" I always tell them, "Get yourself a different advisor!"

Small Town Lessons --- Global consequences

It seems anywhere you look today there's news about the global economy. There's no getting around it--- the leaders of the majority of countries went and got themselves into a huge mess by borrowing too much money in order to try to grow their respective economies and keep their political careers in motion.

7

We may live in separate countries, but the whole global economy is affected by any financial crisis to a few members. It's a delicate balance.

This book isn't about how to fix the banks in Greece, Italy or one of dozens of South American nations. It's not about the dangers of a failing Chinese stock market. I'm not saying the issues abroad aren't worthy of attention, but not what we are writing about in my book.

Coming from a hardworking town in Southeastern Arizona I was aware of the financial stature of the majority of people there. Most were simple, hardworking folk, and what they did earn they definitely wanted to keep. I grew up very aware that if you made a mistake with your investments prior to retirement, it wasn't going to make for a comfortable lifestyle.

I learned that my best clients --- the ones I most enjoyed working with --- were those who understood the concept of **Enough.** They knew what their unique parameters were for not what they necessarily wanted----but what they had and what they needed.

They were **Content**. They were **Debt Free**. Most importantly, they had **Peace of Mind**.

Can you depend on Retirement Plans to guarantee a financially safe future?

Let's take a deeper look at 401(k) and other retirement plans (TSPs, IRAs, 403Bs or Deferred Comp 457s) that are funded with risk investments and find out why they make money for everybody involved with the plan - except the poor schnook who's putting his hard-earned money in.

Sure you thought you were contributing to your own retirement future. Instead, for the last twenty-plus years, you've probably been contributing to the comfortable retirements for a whole lot of people in the financial services industry who made money whether you did or not!

From the mid-1980s to the present, Wall Street invited you and millions of other Americans to a game when billions of 401(k) dollars were put into the stock market ... and the real estate market. Wall Street executives should have known better. They should have known that mortgage-backed securities, which boosted the real estate market from 1999 to 2007, were potentially toxic in a real estate downturn --- the down cycles that occur every ten to twelve years since 1945! They likely saw the collapse of the real estate bubble coming. But they didn't say a thing to us about the risk that the mortgage-backed securities

9

would have on the U.S. and international stock markets and Wall Street firms. Instead, brokers encouraged further investment in stocks and mutual funds because the party was never going to end.

The party always ends!

What goes up, profits are taken. When stock markets retreat drastically like 2002 & 2008-2009, that is the time to get back in and make money on the way back.

Would you have liked a strategy in which you didn't lose a dime on the way down, and participated in the stock market recovery on the way back up? Well, my clients enjoyed that strategy...... and if you keep reading, so will you!

Why your 401k or other retirement plan that are at risk probably won't let you retire with Peace of Mind

What if your retirement plan incurs the same kind of dramatic losses that happened twice in the last 15 years?

That retirement plan now won't let you retire on time or with the same amount of resources to support your desired lifestyle. We aren't talking about retiring to an epic castle in the south of France overlooking the beach. I know you want to be able to afford to stay in your home, pay for your basic lifestyle expenses, get in some leisure activities like golf or fishing, and have a little leftover to travel abroad or visit those grandkids.

Once that 401(k) or other plan has dropped by 40 percent, that retirement timecard isn't quite ready to punch out.

There are actually two basic reasons why the decisions that will allow you to retire securely are now on your back: 1) the replacement of a company's core retirement program with the 401(k) plan and 2) the greed of Wall Street that drove the economy into the real estate and tech bubbles and other financial meltdowns.

Let's take a look and see how these things played out.

A History of the current Financial Insecurity

From about 1940 to the mid-1980s, people working in the private sector secured their retirement through their company's core pension program. The core program was usually modeled similar to the government's **defined benefits** program, which stated that if you worked X amount of years, you would get Y amount of money as a pension in each year of your retirement. The **defined benefits** program was the deal that currently most federal and state employees like teachers, policemen, and firemen receive.

In the private sector, for employers like XYZ Corporation, it was the company's responsibility to fund and manage the core retirement programs and ensure that these were part of the corporation's assets. The federal government was only a retirement guarantor of last resort if the private company experienced bankruptcy, defaulted, or faced other major financial challenges or setbacks.

The government's bailout of Chrysler back in 1981 was an interesting example of this arrangement. Congress gave $1 billion in loan guarantees to Chrysler to revive its operations when the company was on its last legs. Congress opted to go that route rather than the more costly route of fulfilling its obligation to payout $1.5 billion for the company's pension plan in case of bankruptcy. However, the Chrysler situation was very rare. Until then, most employers funded their pension plans appropriately and paid their retirees what they were owed.

The 401(k) plan was the more prominent supplemental program enacted by Congress in the 1960s and 1970s. There was also the 403(b) plan for those people who worked for public education, churches, and non-profit organizations.

Interestingly enough, from the introduction of 403(b) plans in 1963 to 1993 educators and employees of non-profits could only put annuities into their 403(B) plans. The Kennedy Administration mandated only safe, guaranteed investments for their plans. That changed in 1993 when Congress opened up the 403(B) plans to mutual funds in addition to annuities, often with the same disastrous results for those who shifted from safety to risk when the stock markets tanked.

These payroll-deducted, supplemental programs (IRAs, 401(k), 403(B), 457, etc.) were also called **defined contribution programs**: The Internal Revenue Service (IRS) defined how much you were able to put into those plans in addition to what was put into the core program of your company. The supplemental programs were great programs because they enabled workers to retire and still receive darn near the same amount of money they had received while working.

Even if you didn't have money to put into the supplemental programs, you still had your core program, and you learned to live with what you got. Even when people lost money in the supplemental programs for whatever reason, they would still have the back-up core program and Social Security.

A back-up plan is always good! So what happened?

Why did Congress and the IRS allow Wall Street to take control of your retirement future by shifting the burden for savings away from corporate America and onto the backs of you hard working Americans?

Before we discuss those issues, let's discuss how I developed my *Retirement Endgame* strategies and my passion for safe money retirement planning.

Chapter 2

Re-thinking Risk vs. Reward: My Story & Insights

I know why you ended up on this page: you have money you can't afford to lose, and are looking for a safe exit out of the Wall Street Casino.

Well, a good question is how I ended up writing this book.

I have been in the financial services industry for over 12 years. I've worked for the big boys on Wall Street telling our clients to stay fully invested and at risk. I was trained to educate our clients that without Risk there was no Reward.

Over the last 12 years I witnessed one of the greatest financial catastrophes since the 1930s. I saw people's financial lives completely flipped over ---- their personal lives disrupted because they couldn't retire as they previously planned --- their relationships strained from the layoffs, lost retirement funds, and overall stress of uncertainty.

What about my clients?

They didn't lose a dime using my Retirement Endgame strategies during 2008-2009. They have made a good return on their retirement accounts, and their futures are secured by the foundational principles I will outline in Chapter 4.

They don't panic when the markets have huge corrections like in October 2014, January 2015, and August 2015. They know their nest egg is safe!

They don't call me for my latest stock tips or other "can't miss investment ideas.

Why? Because my clients aren't ruled by **Fear and Greed.**

They are ruled by their desire for Peace of Mind and Financial Wisdom.

Small Town Perspective with the Big Picture in Mind

I was born and raised in a sleepy little town in southeast Arizona. Neither parent had the proverbial silver spoon passed down to them. They were middle class, hard-working folk who gained my admiration for their sacrifices that allowed me to pursue my passion for sports.

I grew up outside of town in the country where I learned to work hard from a young age. I discovered from that hard work one basic fact that motivated me throughout my life: **if you want to make it in this world, work hard and don't look for any shortcuts!**

I had to feed all the chickens, goats and turkeys before breakfast. It was one of the great memories of growing up: the chores and learning discipline at a young age. I had a very close family, including my parents, and two younger sisters.

There were no video games and social media that so occupy children's free time today. We enjoyed the old-fashioned lifestyle of outdoor recreation. My parents were always so very positive with us kids and wanting more for us than they ever had. My parents were very hardworking people that woke up early to work and give us all they could. They impressed us to be Leaders, not Followers.

All the years of hard work in my developing years gave me a great hunger to succeed in all I did throughout my school years. I wanted to make my parents proud of me and to know that all their sacrifices would not be wasted on a half-ass effort in my pursuits. I had a thirst to win, and an attitude that said, "If you're gonna do something, you might as well be the best you can be!"

It didn't matter what the sport, school project or competition. Maximum effort to achieve success was the goal, and failure wasn't an option. I'm proud to able to say that I was a small town kid who worked hard and was able to accomplish everything I was ever involved in order to represent my family in a positive light.

I had a heck of a sports career in high school playing Varsity football, wrestling, and track & field all four years --- which is pretty rare in any part of the country. Those sports and my good academics took me to college where I played two sports, and received All-American honors --- not once --- but twice in my collegiate career.

So I hope you get the picture. My current competition is the Wall Street Casino and their misinformation machine. I'm here to educate you, keep your money safe, and guide you to a secure retirement---- and I won't fail you or me!

I have always seen that successful people share common traits, such as discipline and perseverance. A winner digs deep and guts it out when others quit and want to lie down and feel bad for themselves. I am not a person that has ever laid down and I really don't even like to sit down. I feel that the resiliency that I've been able to utilize to overcome challenges in sports and my financial services career were born out of a work ethic infused into me from childhood. All those challenges that I have gone through and overcome in sports and financial services through that Great Recession stem from hard work infused into my being from childhood.

There's a reason 75% of Wall Street imploded in 2008-2009 downturn: The Wall Street Casino lacked integrity and it lacked honesty. That's why most of the people I know who sold risk investments for their client's "can't afford to lose" retirement plans were out of business, along with the mortgage crowd.

They lacked common sense and integrity. They didn't do for people what they would have wanted done for them.

I was blessed to receive a full ride scholarship to a great college. I have been blessed with great clients over the past twelve years. And I'm blessed that you are reading this book!

Let's be honest: I busted my backside in sports, and ditto in financial services. Grit and grind is in my DNA.

I tend to gravitate to seek out those people who have worked hard to save for retirement, and who need me to direct them to financial security.

Whether my client is a friend or family member, I have the confidence that I will be able to look them in the eye and confirm that they won't lose money ---- and that in the future have a wonderful, stress-free retirement.

I want the same for you!

The Retirement Endgame was written for the person who knows that they're in the Casino, but need an alternative strategy to maximize their growth without stock market risk, stress, and their advisor's constant coin-flipping as to what to do next.

After you have worked hard to accumulate your nest egg, you must realize that losses hurt more than gains help. You don't have 10-20 years to recover your financial future when your advisor tells you to stay the course --- and the market takes another dump!

My safe money strategies not only help people get to retirement, but maximizes the most effective tax strategies to receive income when you get to there.

Risk vs. Reward:

The Fallacy of the Wall Street Mantra

Before we move on, let me set something straight: I'm not anti-Stock Market! My strategies allow my clients to participate in the growth of the Stock Markets.

My clients are never invested IN the Stock Markets! Their principal is never at risk!

My niche is to work with 95% of people in this country who have two primary assets that will dictate the quality of their retirement lifestyle: **their retirement plans and their real estate equity.**

As we all found out the hard way, both of these assets were tragically exposed to disaster during the Great Recession of 2008-2012.

My advisory practice strategically places about 70-75% of your money into guaranteed principal savings programs, and the other 25-30% in conservative growth funds.

If you follow my *Four Pillars of a Worry-free Financial Plan* in Chapter 4, you will achieve a successful preparation for retirement, and great Peace of Mind during retirement.

Chapter 3

Understanding How Retirement Plans Work

Let's go back and readdress the question I posed at the end of Chapter 1. **Why did Congress and the IRS allow Wall Street to take control of your retirement future by shifting the burden for savings away from corporate America and onto the backs of you hard working Americans?**

The Retirement Plan Dilemma

The key concept is that the corporate 401(k) plan and 403(b) plans for educators and government workers were *never intended to be primary retirement plans*! They were intended to be *supplemental*—to add to what your employer gave you in the core pension plan. Then things changed. In the early 1980s, Congress, the accounting industry, the Wall Street lobbyists, the mutual fund lobby, and the 401(k) plan administrator lobby got together and decided that it was too hard for corporations to fund core retirement programs. Their reasoning probably included the following points:

1) Why use the resources of the corporation to manage a retirement program when workers can do it themselves?

2) We need somebody to buy the common stocks of the companies for which we underwrite; why not have millions of corporate workers become the buyers?

They concluded that corporate workers should have a 401(k) plan where they would put a portion of their incomes in Wall Street investments that are supposed to grow to fund their retirement instead of a company's core retirement plan. So the 401(k) plan went from being a supplemental plan to becoming *the primary retirement* vehicle for millions of American workers. Corporations only had to partially match the worker's contributions—that is, if the worker could even afford to contribute. The companies then forced the employee to remain with the company 3, 5, or 10 years in order to be eligible to be vested to that employer match.

Through the urging of different highly compensated Wall Street and 401(k) lobbyists, private sector companies like Ford, Chrysler, and several of the largest domestic airlines decided to be rid of their core retirement programs and set up 401(k) plans for their workers. Over the next twenty-five years, more and more companies eliminated their core retirement programs while the state, county, and city governments retained them for their employees. Currently, fewer than 30 percent of American companies still have core retirement programs. The responsibility of funding retirement has slowly been shifting and placed on the backs of private sector workers—people like Fred.

Workers were sold on the 401(k) idea originally because we were told that we would have more control over our retirement money. The 401(k) salesmen told us, "Wouldn't it be better to control your own retirement account? You could put money in stocks, bonds, or mutual funds, and probably do better than whatever your company's core retirement plan offers. You can tailor your own plan to your own risk tolerance. Think of it! You can be in control of your own destiny! Of course, we'll charge a fee or two for all that ... but still! You'll be the boss!"

How much control did workers really have? Did they have control over the fact that they lost money in stocks, bonds, and mutual funds in the 1987 stock market crash, during the recession of the early 1990s, during the tech bubble that burst around 2001, or during the recent economic meltdown? They had no control at any of those times!

In addition, how much control did workers really have over where they could invest their money through their 401(k) plans? They could only invest in stocks, bonds, and mutual funds that *paid commissions and fees to financial services firms and funds.* You couldn't stick your 401(k) money in any truly safe, risk-free investment like CDs or fixed insurance annuities. Why not?

Because if you did, no one on Wall Street could make money off of you!

Would you like to put your 401(k) money in a bank CD? That's an investment guaranteed by the FDIC. Well, somehow, the 401(k) lobbyists and the rest of the Wall Street lobbyists excluded bank CDs from 401(k) plans. In fact, the lobbyists got Congress to say that we can't have products that have a *back-end surrender charge* (or a charge for pulling out funds before the completion of a certain period of time such as five years) on the menu for your investments. Wouldn't you know it? CDs have back-end surrender charges! Fixed annuities have back-end surrender fees! What a coincidence! The lobbyists probably used this justification: "We were just trying to protect Americans from getting charged on their investments in case they changed their minds or needed their money for unforeseen emergencies."

Well, so much for protection! While Wall Street was convincing Congress to set down these favorable restrictions for 401(k) plans (favorable to Wall Street!) in the early 1980s, CDs and fixed annuities earned 12 to 14 percent annually without risk, while the stock markets were hovering at Depression-era levels (adjusted for inflation). Wall Street desperately needed to figure out a way to bail itself out of a depressed market. It succeeded with the newfound supply of funds to purchase stocks and mutual funds through the 401(k) plans of the American worker.

When a downturn happens, you might ask, "Why are there no safe options in my retirement plan?" The harsh but simple answer is that Wall Street doesn't want Safe options like CDs and annuities because they won't make any money that way. If you can't use bank CDs and annuities for your 401(k) account, you are stuck with the tried and true casino games provided by Wall Street. With a fee here and a charge there, Wall Street firms stood to benefit enormously from 401(k) plans. And they did. They made millions and millions of dollars from charging your investment account, whether or not you made money.

So we see that the replacement of a company's core retirement plan was to Wall Street's financial benefit. They now receive money that was yours at one time; however, you bear all the risk—not your corporation (Wall Street's partner in crime is the company, who historically had to fund your retirement with conservative investments).

The Wall Street casino could take a devastating toll on 401(k) investments, even if the average Joe thinks that he played his cards right. Here is a rough summary of how the process works. A Wall Street firm goes to a company and says, "Hey, let us raise money for you by selling an interest in your company called a common stock." When a company agrees, the Wall Street firm has to sell the stock to somebody in order to raise funds for development and growth. Why not stick some stocks in mutual funds into your 401(k) account as you contribute monthly to your plan under the direction of your plan's brokerage custodian? After all, you checked a box that indicated you had some tolerance for risk! Just how much risk are you bearing? Well, if you buy the stock or shares of the mutual fund, you own 100 percent of the risk of the stock if it loses value. And you don't even know you bought the stock because your fund managers bought the stock for him. So the risk of the company's stock is borne not by the sharks on Wall Street but by the minnows on Main Street.

Mutual fund companies have a huge desire to purchase common stocks with the money in people's 401(k) accounts under their management. The fund advisors will call their investors like you and ask if you would like to invest in a utility fund that contains stocks from AT&T or Southern California Edison, tech funds, healthcare funds, or real estate funds. Wall Street is thrilled that mutual funds are doing billions of dollars of transactions in 401(k) accounts and taking not-too-informed orders from people like you.

The average Joe doesn't really know if he is investing in the right companies. He is just listening to the advice of his advisors—

who could be the low-paid clerks at the brokerage firm handling millions of inquiries nationwide or your buddies in the lunchroom. You look at the menu of investments and say, "Well, why don't I put some money in the Dow Jones, the S&P, this healthcare fund and that tech fund ..." You pick those investments with the same confidence you'd have trying to pick horses at the track; you choose based on the bookie's information or "tout" sheets, the color of the jockey's shirt, or the lucky number of the horse?

Before 1982, less than 5 percent of the U.S. population owned stocks. Since 401(k) plans went from being supplemental to being the main retirement vehicle for millions of Americans. The biggest holders of stocks in this country are average Joes of the world, the people who hold 401(k) and other retirement accounts. Today, state pension funds such as the California Public Employees' Retirement System (CalPERS) have $215 billion invested, and 75 percent of the money is in stocks. (I was told by some actuaries of several state public employee pension funds, teachers' funds, and military funds that their funds need to make about 6 to 7 percent a year for a period of time in order to adequately fund everyone's retirement over time—40 percent drops are devastating to them and ultimately to taxpayers who must bail out those retirees!) Add to that the amount invested in the corporate stocks from other pension and mutual funds, and you witness an explosion in the stock market since the early '80s.

With the proliferation of 401(k) plans, stocks were sold at a higher volume, and they also had greater volatility—they could swing up or down more quickly with the emotional knee-jerk tendencies of the investing public. Before the explosion, the Dow Jones Industrial Average was at 800 in 1982. These numbers turn out to be lower than the Dow in the 1930s when adjusted for inflation. However, as 401(k) plans gained popularity from 1983 on, we saw the Dow Jones go as high as 14,000 by October 2007 and then back down to 6,500 just eighteen months later (a loss of 53 percent) as we all painfully witnessed in early 2009. Even though the markets have doubled off their March 2009 lows, they are still, at this writing, only up 25 percent above their peaks of 2007.

Your participation, along with the participation of millions of other average folks, generated huge demand for common stocks. From 1984 to 1987, stocks grew in price. The Dow went from 800 in 1982 to over 2600 in 1987. Wall Street was elated because its firms made 2.5 percent and 3 percent annually in fees off your money invested in retirement plans ... whether you made money or not. And the mutual funds and brokerage firms make *25 to 30 percent of your account value over a ten-year period* from your money peddling risk. Further subtract the bite of taxes on your gains, and you're lucky to be left with a 50 percent net of your imagined gains!

However, there's a reason why stocks are considered risky—there is always the chance that you will lose big. All of a sudden, in October 1987, the Dow dropped 33 percent in two weeks from 2600 to 1739. That was, to say the least, devastating!

Before that crisis, a lot of people who bought stocks borrowed against the rising value of their stocks to buy new houses or cars, take vacations, and invest in businesses. They might have borrowed up to 70 or 80 percent of the value of stock portfolio. These people woke up one day and discovered their stocks were down about 30 percent. Then came many margin calls: Brokers demanded that these investors put more money in their portfolios or sell some assets to make up the loss. Many people got wiped out in late 1987 because of the added pressure of folks having to sell their stocks when they didn't have more cash to put into their accounts.

After that experience, people wanted to be more careful, so it took several years before the market returned to a bullish attitude. Then around the mid-90s, we saw a buying frenzy stoked by a Wall Street-created bubble in the tech industry. The bubble involved thousands companies that had no sales, no revenues, and no earnings per share. Wall Street analysts made up stories about the viability of these companies. All of a sudden, you called your brokerage firm, whether it was Fidelity or Schwab or another large firm, and you asked, "What's up? What's hot?" And they would tell you about the tech stocks. You might then rush to get out of the secure blue-chip stocks and jump into the tech stocks, investing $100,000 or even over a million dollars because you didn't want to miss the boat! As always, it's your *fear* of missing the gains or getting the losses versus Wall Street's *greed* for making money whether you do or not—and all of it fueled by *worry* created by Wall Street's engine of misinformation.

From 2000 to 2003, the stock market went down 50 percent because in the late '90s it was obsessed with tech stocks that had absolutely no value. Probably 80 percent of tech companies involved in the bubble went out of business, and investors lost the majority of their investments. The 401(k) account holders got cleaned out of a boatload of money from 2000 to 2003. How could I even put people's anger into words? That would take another book!

From 2003 to mid-2007, the market finally got back to where it was in early 2000: it gained 60 percent off its 2002 lows. Guess what folks we had a new bubble; this time it was called real estate. Once again Wall Street fueled the engine of *greed*. Real estate grew so dramatically during that time that Wall Street got together with the banks and created instruments called "Collateralized Debt Obligations" (CDO's). Wall Street said to the banks, "Hey, we've got a great deal for you. Put together as many loans as you can—hundreds of thousands of them. We'll break them up, package them, and sell them to pension funds, mutual funds, foreign governments and the general public in their 401(k) plans. You make huge fees and bonuses—we make huge fees and bonuses—and guess who assumes all the risk for this new casino game?"

This CDO party went on for years, and things got so overheated that lending institutions loaned money to people who could not have qualified for a loan under normal, prudent underwriting standards. Now, many of these people qualified for a loan for home purchases by just having a pulse! Nearly everyone qualified for a home loan from 2000 to 2007 as the lax underwriting of the greedy lenders didn't even check to see if they had jobs!

For example, at the insistence of Congress during 2002-2007 to help low-income families to partake in the explosion in real estate prices, loans were made available to people in low-income communities in Southern California and other parts of the country who could not afford to repay those loans. It seems that nobody at any of the lending institutions involved in peddling the mortgage-backed CDOs did the basic prudent mortgage underwriting or reality checks to ensure that the people to whom they lent were able to qualify and repay the loans. Easy money always creates an over-bought environment—whether in stocks or real estate!

Wall Street likes to keep pushing stocks until the end of the line even after the firms made their fees, executives exercised their stock options, and the analysts received their bonuses. The real estate bubble fueled easy money, easy credit, and improper underwriting. Now banks like Countrywide (now B of A), WaMu (now Chase), IndyMac and Wachovia (now Wells Fargo) are bailed out for Wall Street's and the lender's greed after 401(k) holders lost 40 to 50 percent of their money in the stock market, while seeing their real estate values plunge 30-40 percent in just two short years. So the executives of the lending institutions and Wall Street got theirs—but what about you? You guessed it ... you're left holding the bag, a bag which contains about 40 percent less money than it did a year ago!

Some firms were also pushed to the edge of sanity. Follow me closely on this one. The giant insurer AIG thought it was taking advantage of an opportunity and getting a piece of the CDO pie when it proposed to reinsure the market value of mortgage securities to the institutional investors who bought them. Wall Street responded, "Great! Now we have an exit strategy for an overheated market." Suddenly, when the real estate bubble burst and investors of CDOs lost money, AIG had to honor insurance contracts for the purchasers of the mortgage securities. AIG couldn't honor all the contracts because even though it had assets, it didn't have time to sell off other assets to obtain the cash to pay its reinsurance obligations on those toxic mortgage pools. AIG formed a new game in the Wall Street casino, and it lost.

Before the bubble, the AIG life insurance and annuity divisions were (and continue to be) as solid as they can be. AIG made hundreds of millions of dollars in fees on insurance and annuity premiums. So it didn't need to play the CDO game, but it did so because of greed. The U.S. government had little choice but to bail out AIG because the company was so big that its failure might have taken down the entire global economy. But where's your bailout? Nowhere, of course!

AIG has already paid off their Government loans, which shows the strength of the insurance industry compared to the still dead Wall Street firms.

After the real estate bubble had burst in mid-2007, there was a lot of finger pointing. The truth is the real estate bubble represented a new game of chance that formed in the Wall Street casino. Organizations such as AIG and WaMu participated in the game of chance, and everyone lost this time—not just you, but only you took a lasting hit. The Federal Reserve was never going to bail you out! Instead, what was left of your hard-earned cash (turned into tax dollars) was used to bail out the very institutions that had nearly destroyed the economy in the first place!

When 401(k) and Wall Street lobbyists convinced Congress and the Department of Labor during the 1980s that CDs and life insurance annuities (which guarantee principal during accumulation and a lifetime income) weren't a good idea for your menu of investment options for your 401(k) plan, they were not looking out for your interest. Now you call your advisor, who is one of those good-old boys on Wall Street, and say, "I'm 65 years old. I can't afford to lose any more money. What options have you got for me?"

The only option that the advisor has for you is to put your money in bond funds, which are considered less risky than stock funds. But just how safe are bond funds? During the stock market debacle of 2008 and 2009, the average bond fund went down *15 percent*. It is absolutely criminal that you have no safe options! Compared with stock funds, it was slightly less of a beating, but was it justifiable? No way!

Let's take another look back in history. As we discussed earlier, the stock market was so bad during the 1930s recession that it took about 25 years, until 1954, for the Dow-Jones

Industrial Average to get back to where it was in 1929. In fact, if you had put your money in a bank or other conservative investment that only gave you 4.7 percent per year, you would have matched the performance of the Dow from 1929 to 1973! Now, you might ask yourself, what's the point of trying to pick the best funds and the best stocks in the first place if all I needed along the way is just a 4.7 percent annual return on my investments? Good question! It sure isn't worth the lost sleep and ulcers!

From 1996 to 2003, only 24 percent of mutual fund managers outperformed the leading indexes—NASDAQ, S&P 500, and Dow Jones. Doesn't it make more sense to just put money in the indexes through no-load mutual funds and let them do what they do instead of spending all that time, money, and resources trying to find the next hot fund or market sector? Study after independent study proves that you will beat the professionals 76 percent of the time! Wouldn't your bookie like those odds?

Since 2003, 90 percent of professionals did not beat the indexes. In addition, even in desperate times, financial advisors were *still* not giving advice in their clients' best interest. In 2007 and 2008, financial advisors actually encouraged people to go into the Chinese and Indian stock markets when things started slowing down in the American market. Once people set foot into Asian waters, they drowned, and their stocks went down 60 percent while our market went down 50 percent. It's almost like the financial advisors ensured that you didn't miss the opportunity to lose more money in the Chinese casino!

In a segment that aired in the spring of 2009, Steve Kroft from CBS's *60 Minutes* interviewed the leading 401(k) plan lobbyist to Congress and asked how they could allow these losses to happen. He smugly answered that the problem wasn't created by the 401(k) administration industry; the problem lies with the *investment community*! In other words, Wall Street!

The lobbyist also stated that people like you *should have known* that you were putting money at risk when you put money in your 401(k) mutual funds. With that answer, Steve Kroft's mouth dropped open. Where was the conscience in that answer? How do the financial wizards of Wall Street sleep at night, disavowing any responsibility for having destroyed the retirement dreams of the millions of investors who trusted them?

The bottom line is that even though the stock market has begun to rise again after this devastating loss of wealth, don't get too excited. You are still charged fees. Your money is still at risk. Chances are that *the market will never go up enough to recoup the losses you suffered in the past—especially if you don't have a lock-in mechanism to handle the possibility of future downturns.* In addition, Wall Street will most certainly come up with another market-frenzied bubble, maybe this time in commodities like oil or metals that certainly should go up because of the devaluation of our currency after the extreme increase of the money supply by the Fed to prevent a global meltdown. Wall Street will regenerate the public's appetite for risk and entice Congress to stay the course with the present 401(k) plan structure instead of allowing the public to shift their 401(k) menu options to safe savings programs prior to age fifty-nine and a half.

We can only conclude that Wall Street and their 401(k) system is just one vicious shark frenzy tank. Millions of average Joes are dropped into the tank but don't know why they are in the tank or how they got there. That's why you will never be able to retire with peace of mind from possible future catastrophic losses...as long as the current flawed investment system remains in place.

So if the 401(k) plan doesn't work, what will? What do you really need in order to create a retirement that Wall Street can't destroy? You need three things: *knowledge, understanding,* and *control* over your own retirement savings. You need to have the flexibility of being able to invest in safe money options not offered by your employer's 401(k) plan.

I'll now describe for you **The Retirement Endgame's** safe money alternatives so you can learn how to protect your money. For all you average Joes, if you're reading, I have good news.

It's not too late to save your retirement dreams ... if you take the advice you'll find in the next chapter.

Chapter 4

The Four Pillars of a Worry-Free Financial Plan

In this chapter, I want to share with you the foundation of my **Retirement Endgame** strategies. It rests on four principals or pillars, so you can clearly see the strength of the system and why it can last forever. Taking the worry out of financial planning is one of my greatest gifts to my clients. I'm not performing magic. I'm just following the four-pillar investment approach of the safe money philosophy, and I'd like to describe them for you now. The four pillars of safe money are as follows:

1) Guarantee the safety of your principal

2) Control and flexibility of your money

3) A crediting method for growth on your money based on participation in the stock market gains, but not the losses

4) A lock-in mechanism that secures the growth of your account value to prevent losses during a future downturn.

Let's see how each of these will have a highly positive effect on your financial life.

The First Pillar: Guarantee

In today's world, most people think of the idea of **guaranteed principal** as wishful thinking. What do you mean, "guaranteed principal?" Get out of town! It's impossible! The idea is almost bizarre to people who have lost large amounts of their principal in the stock market. So it takes a while for me to convince some of these individuals that it *is* possible to have a lucrative investment in which the principal is completely protected and completely guaranteed.

People were led to believe by Wall Street that in order to have a proper or aggressive return on their investment, they must be involved in some risk. In fact, society now correlates risk directly with return: More risk equals more return. If someone doesn't want to bear risk, he is considered the social outcast—the bench-sitter. He's ostracized socially. All his friends at the club brag about the risky nature of their investments because somehow that translates in their minds into being bold, swaggering, and success oriented. Can you hear Wall Street asking you, "What's the matter, not tough enough?"

Of course, it never occurs to people that the "risk" part of the risk/reward equation might actually happen to them and that they will lose some or most of their hard-earned money. The

41

reality is they sure have in the last couple of years. Now they aren't bragging about risk anymore!

Now that risk is a little less desirable, what types of investments exist that guarantees the safety of the principal? Investors who choose to avoid risk have limited options on Wall Street. They can either invest in CDs or bonds—products that don't yield much return. Consequently, less return means less money to retire on. If that happens to you, then you should be afraid, very afraid. By investing in CDs or bonds, you're really guaranteeing yourself losses—because the meager rate of return on those investments will never keep pace with inflation. That's especially true in light of the greater inflation rates we can all expect in years to come.

Wall Street knows that deep down many investors are gamblers and actually *crave* risk. They prey on our fears that we won't have enough and that safe investments are all doomed to failure. (At least, the safe investments *they* offer are doomed!) So their ads, which appear to focus on offering you a great retirement through their investment products, are really intended to induce fear. If Wall Street succeeds in inducing fear in you, then they succeeded in their marketing and sales campaign to get you to invest in risky securities with them.

The big investment companies want clients to fear that they aren't making enough money so they have to invest with more risk, or that they will lose money if they don't invest and thus miss a golden opportunity. I don't call watching the Dow sliced in half in a matter of months a golden opportunity for investors, but they don't worry about your returns as long as you place your money under their control. Instead, they want you to fret that the train is leaving the station; you are either on it too late or too soon. If you are on it too soon, you should have waited for more risk to come along before getting on board with your investments. If you are on it too late, you watch everyone else make money while you are left behind. Either way, Wall Street wins by getting your money. The bottom line is that Wall Street has to continually inject worry into the mindset of the public.

Every time you jump into the risk wagon with Wall Street, it's going to dump a lot of "wastepaper securities" on you. I define wastepaper securities as "the investments that knowledgeable investors are too smart to fall for." With this trend of "you jumpin' and them dumpin'," it is not a surprise that the principal you put into your investments is almost guaranteed ... to deteriorate if not evaporate altogether. When deterioration happens, people begin to lose hope of ever finding financial products that would guarantee a safe principal.

Now is the time that we pick ourselves up from the ashes and look for financial products that satisfy our first Safe Money requirement of guaranteed principal. We covered the first steps in the previous chapters: doing your history homework to see what kinds of returns are *realistic*; finding the financial products that could get you those returns; and most importantly, protecting your principal investment. In addition, we have to understand what kinds of cycles and bubbles exist on Wall Street that would backfire on the investments we make and what kinds of products could be immune from the same dangers.

Guaranteed principal is a must-have necessity to ensure that you have enough money with which to retire. You contribute to your retirement funds year after year and delay gratification so that you can enjoy life later. You shouldn't let Wall Street make your efforts worthless.

As we've seen, the one investment that definitely guarantees your principal is a fixed index annuity. My clients have never experienced a loss of their principals with this approach. Their principals are guaranteed by the financial strength of some of the largest, most stable insurance companies in the world, such as Allianz Life, National Western, Athene, and Nationwide.

Over the last 120 years, no policyholder of a life or annuity contract has lost one dime of their original principal on their savings plans with these companies. They are rated by AM Best, Standard and Poor's, and Moody based on the quality of their investment portfolio (which is primarily in investment grade bonds and government securities and mortgages) and by how much surplus over potential claims they have. All of the companies mentioned above (and most other A-rated or better companies) have between 130-160 percent surplus cash to potential claims for cash redemptions on their life and annuity policies. How much surplus do you think your bank has? Zero, and that's why they need the FDIC to cover any liquidity problems when there's a run on the bank!

The guarantees for my clients are not only on the original savings principal but also on the future account values that have grown from interest crediting. During the negative years in the stock market, my clients make nothing, but during the positive years, they make about 60 percent of the gains made on Wall Street. Their gains are also locked-in along with their principal to prevent losses down the road as they approach retirement so that their lifetime incomes will not be diminished. We will discuss the importance of this lock-in mechanism later on.

The Second Pillar: Control and Flexibility

Now let's turn to the second core aspect of the safe money philosophy: **the issue of control and flexibility.** Having control and flexibility over your retirement planning isn't just about having a 401(k) plan but also about controlling your real estate portfolio and your other savings programs. In addition, you also control "nonqualified" assets such as money obtained from inheritances or properties you may have sold. Even though these assets are nonqualified because they are not directly in your retirement fund, they are still part of the stash of cash from which you will live in the future.

Every asset you accumulate over the course of your lifetime should be viewed as continually flowing into a large pot of money from which you will draw your retirement income. For most folks, the two largest assets used to accumulate a retirement nest egg are their Qualified retirement plan (IRA, 401(k), TSP, 403(b), etc.) and their real estate. The ultimate goal of all our investments is to have a pot of money down the road that provides more income than our budget needs.

I always define "wealth" as having more money coming in from savings and investments when you retire than what's going out to pay your budget necessities—without having to work or receive Social Security or other assistance from family! The shame is that only 5 percent of Americans fall into this definition.

We have a lot of different things in our pot of money that we need to control and manage. Nowadays, 60 percent of that needed pot of money is no longer located in our employers' core retirement plans since, as we've seen, most of the core plans have been replaced by 401(k)s. As a result, our control and flexibility over our retirement money is reduced because 401(k)s are managed by somebody else. Unfortunately, that "somebody" is the Wall Street Casinos. Since you've read this far, you know that can't be good for you!

Let's take a quick moment to describe what I mean by control and flexibility over your savings and investments. Control is the ability to liquidate or refinance the asset WHEN you need it—not when or at the dictates of the market or economy! In other words, you have no control (and therefore no flexibility) over your savings or net worth if you don't know what the account or asset will be worth at a future time when needed or if you are unable to make a phone call and receive the funds in a timely manner.

If your money is "buried in your backyard" as real estate equity and you need cash fast for emergencies or income needs, you have to ask your banker for YOUR money—and then hope the economic climate isn't like the situation in 2008 or 2009 when you do so. Nothing is more upsetting than witnessing someone who was diligent in paying off all or most of their home who needs cash to pay bills when they lose a job, get disabled, or become sick and the lender says "Yeah, I know the money's buried in the backyard, but you can't qualify to pay it back!" this is further discussed in the Chapter on managing your real estate equity.

Also, good luck getting a sell order into your broker to get out of the stock market when it's in a free fall during a panic. The government can shut down the stock markets for a week to cool things down, and who knows what your stocks will be worth after it reopens.

Another vital aspect of controlling your money is this: *Never invest in a limited partnership or any passive investment that limits your access to the money when you might need it or want out for a better opportunity.* You may be giving money to people who may be unable to run a successful business venture or who have no control over economic variables like housing or energy recessions, high inflation, terrorism, or natural disasters. But they sure can give a good sales pitch about why you should invest with them and trust their ability to make you as much money as they'll make upfront off you. Moreover, when the company run by the general partners fails, you won't be able to get your money out because, as limited partner, you do not have liquidity or a say in the financial decisions that affect your money. For example, some real estate and oil and gas limited partnerships in the mid-1980s and early 1900s failed and drained their investors' money. These were put together by huge Wall Street entities! The limited partners could do nothing but wait for the destruction to settle and see if there was anything left after the class action suits were filed. They got pennies on their hard-earned dollars. These investors weren't stupid people. They were doctors and lawyers and other professionals…who got taken for a ride on Wall Street.

The lesson I've sought to impart throughout this book is ***never relinquishing control of your finances to other people.*** When you allow someone else to be in charge of your money, someone like a broker at a major Wall Street firm, you abdicate responsibility for your own future well-being. You need to call the shots on not only your 401(k) plan's investment decisions but also all your other assets because everything you have contributes to your retirement pot.

Remember that if you cannot make a call and receive your money in a timely manner when you need it, you have no control. If you are unable to tap the cash buried in your "backyard" or your rental properties for emergencies, you are not in control of your money—the bank is!

The Third Pillar: Long Term - Low Risk

Now let's examine the third pillar of the Safe Money strategy: **participation in long-term stock market performance without stock market risk.**

Historically, the stock market will give us 6 to 8 percent annual returns over a period of fifteen to twenty years, not the 10 to 15 percent that most brokers tout in their sales pitch. Moreover, we don't know which periods of time will give us only 5 percent and which periods will give us 10 percent. We don't know when the next big storm will be that could wipe all our investments clean. These storms (defined as at least 30 percent declines) happened in 1972-1975, 1981-1984, the early '90s, 2000-2002, and recently in 2007-2009. Anyone with a lick of business common sense knows that cyclical storms interrupt periods of sustained growth in stocks or real estate, but no one can predict exactly when they will occur. No one but the Fed and the Wall Street bankers knows when the credit markets will dry up yet again, causing the "musical chair panic" called recession.

If we look more closely at the returns that investors received over the last decade or so, we will see that most are no better off than they were in 1996, adjusted for inflation. That's what happens when you have two fifty percent drops in the stock market.

Let's take a look at Cindy, who put some money into the stock market in 1996. She made 85 percent on her money from 1997 to 2000. Then she lost it all the growth and some of her principal with the 46 percent market decline during the tech bubble from 2000-2002. Wait a minute! How does a 46 percent loss wipe out my 85 percent gain? Well, her $100,000 in 1996 grew to $185,000 by early 2000. Then the 46 percent loss reduced her account value to $100,000—back to square one, if you will. Remember when I told you that stock losses hurt you more than gains help you?

She regained most of what she lost during 2003-2007 when the markets gained 65 percent, taking her account back to $165,000. Recently, though, in 2007-2009, Cindy lost 45 percent as the overbought real estate and stock market bubble burst. Now, not only has Cindy lost all her gains, but this latest loss took her all the way back to her 1996 account value of around $100,000! It has been a lost thirteen years for Janet.

Had she used my safe money strategies, put her $100,000 into a guaranteed principal account, and only received 4 percent annually, she'd have $170,000 in her account in 2009 after the collapse. This is what many of my clients did, and they received more than 4 percent annually. As my clients look back over the years, do you think they remember the huge gains from 1996-2000 or 2003-2007? No!

However, they know they slept well during the disasters in 2000-2003 and the mid-2007 to 2009, knowing that their money was safe!

And, with the market comeback since 2009, my clients are still ahead of their stock-invested friends because they we're still averaging 6-8% on a higher starting account value ---- and as I'll explain in the next section, they are locked in from future losses unlike their friends exposed to market risk!

When we are looking to invest in financial products, we have to examine things for the long haul. We have to ask questions like *what is the average percent yield over a certain period of time after fees and commissions?* In Cindy's case, the yield came out to zero or perhaps even negative over thirteen years. She might make back some of her money down the road and reclaim an average of 8 to 10 percent average annual return for her investment in stocks, but remember that an 8 percent annual gross yield is only 6 percent after the average annual mutual fund management and broker fees are deducted. A CD or US Treasury bond averaging 4-5 percent would have increased her money by 75 percent over thirteen years. A fixed index annuity would have given her a 6-8 percent annual gain (without management and broker fees) and more than doubled her money over thirteen years—without all the drama, worries, and headaches involved.

Therefore, the safe money strategy promotes products that won't fall short of stock market performance over the long run and, unlike stocks, will provide you with positive and stable returns even in a down stock market. How can that be? Keep reading!

The Fourth Pillar: Lock In your Account Value

The fourth and last safe money pillar centers on the **lock-in mechanism that secures the growth of your account values to prevent losses during a future downturn**. What's the use of having growth on your investment if sometime in the future we hit a down cycle? What's the use of accumulating all those assets when you could lose it all when the music stops, and you don't get to a chair in time? That is why I like products with a lock-in mechanism that secures the gains and ensure that nothing is lost from year to year.

Remember Cindy's bumpy ride with her $100,000 from 1996 to 2009? With the **lock-in mechanism** of the fixed index annuity, she would have not given up her market gains when the sharp declines hit. In fact, using real historic numbers of the S&P 500 index (the index in which Cindy would have participated), she would have doubled her money in thirteen years rather than breaking even with all the stress, and she was only participating in 60 to 70 percent of the market gains—but none of its losses!

Dealing with future higher taxes on your Qualified Plans: A case for Life Insurance

After our discussion of the four pillars of a worry-free financial plan, I want to address some points to supplement your understanding of the safe money strategies.

I need to address the reality of having your qualified retirement accounts like IRAs, TSPs, 403(b)s, or 401(k)s being held hostage by the IRS to an very uncertain tax future.

Where do you think tax rates will be after the additional trillions of dollars that have been thrown at the Wall Street firms, banks, Fannie Mae, and Freddie Mac, and the economy in general to keep them afloat over the last three years? Up? Down? The same?

You know the answer! We have to pay for this deficit mess at some time in the future not to mention funding the huge deficits in Social Security, Medicare, and the looming healthcare crisis! Serving that current $16 trillion debt (and growing) means that tax revenues must increase.

I don't want to have my retirement future held hostage by the IRS when I know that down the road the tax I'll pay will far surpass the benefit I received with my contributions and accumulations. If you get a 25% Federal tax savings on your contribution to your retirement plan, what happens in the future if the IRS raises the marginal tax brackets back to the level of 50-70% like in the pre-1987 years?

You need some options to maximize your future nest egg income as insurance from potentially high taxes to pay all that government debt. Numbers are your friend!

Let's use an illustration because numbers are your friend: A forty-five-year-old investor puts $10,000 into a supplemental retirement program his 403(b), TSP, Deferred Comp 457, or 401(k) plan after the employer match. He gets an 8 percent return a year (about 6.5 percent after fees and commissions) for twenty years from the supplemental saving program. His employer and the government encourage him to do so because the core pension is likely going to be non-existent or at best inadequate to fund the retirement lifestyle equal in income to his working years.

The government gives you monetary incentives to put money into the supplemental program. The government says to you, "Put $10,000 in your retirement fund, and we're going to give you a $3,000 tax savings (assuming you are in a combined 30 percent federal and state tax bracket)." So it only costs you $7000 a year to contribute $10,000. Your accumulated tax savings from the government would come to $60,000 over those twenty years ($3000 per year x 20 years). That sounds really attractive at first, doesn't it? Well, there are multiple ways we can look at this situation that might change your mind.

After twenty years, if you get 8 percent annual returns on your contributions, you would have accumulated $450,000. When you're sixty-five, you'll have some decisions to make. You always had your eye on that second home out in Palm Desert or St. George, Utah. So you want to buy a house, and you cash in. To take your $450,000 out as income, you have to pay 42 percent in combined fed and state taxes (if the tax brackets don't rise). While working, you received a 30 percent Fed and State tax benefit. Now taxes are higher because the lump sum distribution is ordinary income of $450,000 and thus a higher tax bracket. So $450,000 minus 42 percent of $450,000 is $261,000, which is what you actually have in cash to buy your vacation dream home. You just sent the government an $189,000 thank you in one lump payment for their $60,000 tax benefit over the last twenty years. You should ask yourself one question: Whose retirement plan was this after all—mine or Uncle Sam's?

In another scenario, your tax advisor would tell you to take money out "the smart way" over the course of twenty years in retirement rather than a lump sum of $450,000 because you'll be killed in taxes as seen in the previous paragraph. Well, you follow their advice and take out $50,000 annually from your retirement fund from age sixty-six to eighty-five. Now when you withdraw $50,000 annually as income, you get charged 30 percent in taxes because $50,000 (plus all your other Social Security and other income) puts you in the 30 percent combined tax category. So each year you are charged $15,000 in taxes. Over twenty years of payouts, your tax bite grew to $300,000 ($15,000 x 20 years), doing it the "smart way")! But your benefit from the government was still $60,000. Bad plan.

What is a better way to go?

You could pay the IRS its $3,000 a year while they're saving the $10,000 annually for twenty years and not take the government bait—I mean benefit. This way, your loss compared to the other scenarios is minimized. You <u>only</u> pay $60,000 in total taxes over the next twenty to forty years (age forty-five to eighty-five) instead of the much larger numbers in the above scenarios. Why does this make sense?

Well, originally our example showed that you have $10,000 to save per year. With my strategy, you gave $3,000 to the IRS, and now you have $7,000 to save for retirement. It's wiser to keep that $7,000 out of your supplemental retirement fund and choose between the following two safe money strategies:

Strategy A: A properly structured Life Insurance policy

Put $7000 annually into a structured life insurance contract under current IRS parameters that will act like a supercharged Roth account without the IRS's age and income restrictions as to accessibility before age fifty-nine and a half. The benefit is that the buildup of your savings is tax free, meaning that if your savings bring in 5 percent returns this year, this 5 percent will not be taxed.

Another benefit is that withdrawing your money out of the life insurance cash account for pre-retirement emergencies or needs can also be tax-free using loans under current tax law. If you die prior to your desired retirement age, there is a tax-free death benefit for your loved ones that will be substantially more than the after-tax amount of your qualified account.

The math also shows that your monthly income from the life insurance contract would provide an additional 40 percent more monthly income than the traditional qualified plan due to the tax-free loan provisions of the life policy—40 percent more income plus an enhanced death benefit that qualified plans don't give you!

You are able to achieve a comparable 8 percent annual return to the mutual funds in your qualified plan on the cash value of the life policy by using the same indexing strategy I use in the fixed index annuity, including the lock-in of future account values as you near retirement—without the mutual fund risk exposure!

Strategy B: Real Estate for your hedge against inflation

Put that $7000 into investment real estate where you would receive the same tax benefits from depreciation and other expenses as contributing money to a qualified plan. However, you would get more control and flexibility over your money outside of the IRS's restrictions on qualified plans because you can refinance, sell, or hang on to the real estate property. If you have to choose between putting $1,000 in stocks or in real estate (with its leverage), it is better to put the money in real estate for the long haul. I would ask my clients to not give me $1000 to put into a qualified plan or IRA and instead put it in real estate. Ten years down the road, when a downturn happens, you can still sell or refinance your real estate to survive, whereas you would have no control over your stocks shrinking in value.

Your accountant will confirm my numbers on the above illustrations because math is math, and the tax laws are what they are. He or she will not give advice about investments or real estate because they cannot be sure which investments or property purchases are the best for you or what your parameters are. So it is up to you to figure out personal parameters that would affect your real estate decisions on your own, using my advice of seeking balance and contentment for you and your family. We will continue our discussion of real estate and establishing contentment in later chapters.

Trillions of dollars have been thrown into the world economy for bailouts. Decades from now, Americans will likely be paying higher taxes to repay the cost of those bailouts. We need to be again reminded that up till 1987, this country had marginal federal tax brackets as high as 70 percent—plus additional taxes in most states! That fact should get people scratching their heads and saying, "Tell us more about that," or "How did that happen, and will it happen again?" Remember earlier in the book? I explained the importance of your advisor understanding the taxes on your overall planning under a safe money strategy.

The strategies that I have shown work to save you money within all of today's tax laws and give you an idea of how to look at the numbers if tomorrow's tax laws change. The numbers that I shared with you are real. You can't refute them, and you can't argue with them. You must find better investment and savings strategies like my safe money philosophy to help you navigate the tax laws and in the end to be able to finance your retirement dreams.

Chapter 5

Taking Control of Your Retirement Plans

If you read Chapter 3, you know my general feeling about Qualified Plans. I have a strong belief that they aren't necessarily going to get you where you want to go. The primary reason is that, as long as the IRS controls the Qualified Plan—i.e., your IRA, 403(b), 401(k), deferred comp, or Thrift Savings Plan (TSP) - they are essentially holding that money hostage. You can't get at it until you're fifty- nine and a half (or whatever age they decide). And if you try to tap into it before then, you'll be charged additional 10 percent federal plus state penalties for early withdrawal—or possibly more at some unknown tax rate in the future.

You really are held hostage to a future of unknowns. Right now, most people are receiving a tax savings at a rate of 15-25 per-cent on federal tax for their Qualified Plans.

However, is that what the rate's going to be when you start taking it out?

I asked you this question in Chapter 3, and I'm going to ask it again: Where do you think tax rates will go with a current $16.5 trillion federal deficit and no political plan in place to solve it?

You guessed it: **UP!** There's just nowhere else for them to go! Remember those Fram Oil Filter commercials? The tagline was, "Either pay me now or pay me later." You either pay the cost of a filter now, or you pay the cost of a whole freakin' engine later, when your motor seizes because you didn't do the maintenance on your car.

That's exactly what's happening in the current financial crisis. No one can pay now, so the government is going to make us pay later. The IRS can change the rules anytime they want. Like I said in the last chapter, they can raise the age from fifty-nine and a half to sixty-two or sixty-five. They can change the tax brackets; if you're getting a 15-25 percent benefit, they can turn around and make it like it was in the 1980s, when you had up to 70 percent in marginal federal tax brackets.

You think they can't do that? Just watch 'em!

So let's talk about some ways to take control of the money in your Qualified Plans. There are different options available to you, depending on if you're still working or not and how old you are. If you've still got your nose to the grindstone, how do you protect yourself from the Wall Street casino as you accumulate money?

Strategies to Protect your Assets

Before Retirement

The people who are still working fall into two groups: those under fifty-nine and a half, and those over. I'll start by addressing the first group

If you're under fifty-nine and a half and working, and you're still contributing to your retirement accounts, either a 401(k) or another plan, it's imperative that you don't lose any money. But it's tricky because you're stuck with the mutual fund custodian that the company plan has contacted to manage your money — usually one of the large Wall Street custodians. Ten or fifteen years ago, people didn't give that much thought. After 2008, much thought!

If you're over fifty, you really can't afford to lose any money because your working years are numbered. At worst, your qualified money should be in what's called a "balanced" or "blended" mutual fund with stocks and bonds, reducing your risk (in theory) to big corrections in the stock market.

At best, if you're going to retire before age sixty, you need to be in short-term, high-grade corporate or government bonds, because you can't afford to lose any principal.

Corporate or government bonds help you take a little bit

more control of the risk, rather than listening to the custodian's clerks tell you, "Oh, the market always comes back. Go ahead and stay fully invested." Keep in mind that the custodians make the most money when you're fully invested in the stock market and they're netting a juicy income off the annual fees. Those fees are not nearly as high if you're in corporate bonds, and they're even smaller when your money's in a money market account or government bonds.

So that's my advice for the under fifty-nine and a half set.

Now let's talk about if **you're still working and you're fifty-nine and a half** or older. What flexibility do you have to take control of your money in your 401(k), your government TSP, or your teacher's 403(b)?

The answer is: more than you've been told!

Over the last fifteen years we've had two **50 percent drops** in the stock market: between 2000 and 2003, and from late 2007 to early 2009. As we all know, it devastated people's retirement planning nationwide. There were people who were fifty-nine and a half and had planned to retire in the next five to ten years; now they couldn't. They saw their 401(k)s become 201(k)s in the blink of an eye.

What could they have done to protect themselves?

Three words, two hyphens.

It's called an **"in-service, non-hardship distribution"**.

Remember these words! It will protect your financial future!

In 2006, Congress introduced and endorsed this distribution for those employees who were over 59½, still working and who wanted to protect their retirement assets from the Wall Street Casino.

Simply put, it means you can go to your company's plan administrator and say, "How much of my 401(k) or Thrift Savings Plan (Deferred Comp) can I roll over to an IRA and keep working at this company?"

What few of you know is that 90 percent of corporations in the United States allow this. They by law have to tell you how much you can transfer and give you a form with which to do so. You are then allowed to take that money and do a tax-free transfer to an IRA where you now take control of that money with a safe money strategy.

That's great news for you!

It means you can take that money that was previously held hostage in the Casino and buy the savings vehicles that I've proposed in this book, like fixed-index annuities. You can do a self-directed IRA and pay cash for income-producing real estate. It can't be primary real estate or your primary home, but rental property? Sure.

With that self-directed IRA, you can also buy mortgage notes and trust deeds; you can loan money out or buy existing notes or tax liens. Of course you need to discuss these strategies with your financial and tax advisors, but these strategies available to you. They exist in Congressional acts that became part of the IRS code for your benefit and protection—and control.

Now let's talk about the people who change jobs.

You've been laid off, quit, or retired. Let's say you have money in a 401(k) or TSP. You don't need that *in-service, non-hardship distribution*, because you are no longer "in service" now that you aren't working for the company. It might be a scary time for you personally, but the upside is that you have full control to take that 401(k) (or 403(b) or TSP) and roll it over to your own IRA where you can start using my *Retirement Endgame* strategies. You can even go get a new job and start contributing to the new 401(k) plan with new money that comes out of your paycheck.

That old money can be pulled out of the Wall Street casino and put it in safe place, allowing you to build up your own retirement future without the Casino's risk.

Then there are people are who are under fifty-nine and a half and still working, but who need to get out their retirement money for **hardship reasons**. We've been talking about *non*-**hardship distributions**; but what if you have a hardship and you need to get that money?

I've got good news for you all who are under 59 ½ and still working.

There's a provision in the **IRS tax code Section 72T** that allows you to take money out of your retirement account systematically over time. The stipulation? You have to do it for at least five years, *or* until you're fifty-nine and a half.

Let's say you're fifty-three years old. You've got $500,000 in your IRA and you need to get some money out of it, but you don't want to pay the 10 percent early withdrawal penalty to the federal government and whatever the additional penalty is in your state. So what you can do under **IRS Code 72T** is determine what your life expectancy is—if you're fifty-three, it's thirty-two years—and take out, over the next six and a half years, an amount of money subject to your life expectancy that will not be penalized, but will be taxed.

Once you reach fifty-nine and a half, you're done—you can stop taking the money out, or take more money out, or do whatever you want to do. However, for those six and a half years, you can systematically take money out every year to meet your needs.

If you're fifty-six years old, you have to do it for three and a half years before you're fifty-nine and a half. You either have to do it until you're fifty nine and a half, or for a minimum of five years.

If you're in a situation where you need money out of your retirement account, let's talk it over.

These are just a few of the options available to you while you're still working.

Legacy Planning

The last way I help people take control of the money in their Qualified Plan is through **Legacy Planning**. In other words, planning for the kids and grandkids, or your favorite charity. Your legacy is what you leave behind when you depart to the other side of the curtain. It's the way you enrich the lives of the people or institutions you love the most.

You've heard about some of the ways to do this, like a stretch or multi-generational IRA. That's where, at your death, your beneficiaries elect to stretch out the payments of the IRA over their life expectancy, to avoid the big tax hit they would incur if they took it all out in a lump sum as ordinary income. If you have $500,000 in your qualified plan and your spouse is a beneficiary, you can often do a spousal IRA where that money gets transferred over directly to their social security number, without being taxed, and they do with it as they see fit. But if your spouse is deceased and the money goes to your kids or your estate, they have to pay ordinary income tax on that money...unless they elect to stretch out the taxability with a Stretch IRA.

Multi-generational or Stretch IRAs are very popular now, but when my clients tell me they're thinking about it, I ask them the following question: If you're seventy-five and you have a qualified plan, and there's $500,000 to $1 million in this qualified plan, and your beneficiaries are in their fifties, do you really think that they want to take that money over the next thirty-five years?

Different strokes for different folks, but my guess is: **no, they don't!**

It's like winning the lottery. If I win $10 million with a scratch- off card and they tell me, "Okay, you can have $10 million paid over twenty years, or you can have $5 million paid right now," I'm going to take that money now. That way I can manage it and set up my own income so I'm not subject to someone else's rules (not to mention highly volatile economic conditions) for the next twenty years.

So what's an alternative to a Stretch IRA?

RMD (Required Minimum Distribution) Strategies for those over age 70 ½

Let's say you're over age 70 ½. You don't need that qualified money for income, but the IRS forces you to take income with the Required Minimum Distribution (RMD) starting at age 70 ½. You used the safe money strategies to put your money in fixed annuities and life insurance, and you're planning on leaving most of that $500,000 to your kids.

Why not take a five- to ten-year payout and buy a life insurance policy for your kids and grandkids?

This lets you leverage the money in your qualified plan. You get far more money, income tax free, because you were taking money out each year, paying taxes on it, and using the difference to buy a life insurance policy. There will be a big tax-free death benefit to your estate, and you can fund the college education of your grandkids, becoming a huge blessing to your family. This is a lot better than leaving it in a qualified plan that's going to get decimated by taxes down the road.

There's one more safe money strategy for Legacy Planning that I call the "**gifting strategy**." For this strategy, you actually take that money out, pay the tax, then systematically take the balance and gift it. Under current tax law, you are allowed to give $14,000 to each member of your family annually, and your spouse is allowed to do the same.(keep in mind this changes yearly) You do the math—between your kids and grand- kids, that's a lot of money you could be gifting each year!

Plus, you and your spouse are allowed to give millions of dollars each over your lifetimes. (Check for current tax law).

Many of my clients gift a set amount of money to their kids and grandkids each year to fund an Irrevocable Life Insurance Trust (ILIT) so that the death benefit is outside of their estate, not subject to estate taxes that would be due under current tax law if they have an estate over $5 million ($10 million for the couple). Their kids and grandkids will grieve them when they're gone, but they'll also be forever grateful for this incredible gift.

In these strategies, my clients' legacy lives on to continue to bless their heirs!

If any of these ideas interest you, I strongly suggest you make an appointment with my office to discuss them further. My goal is to give you concepts and ideas, to show you a world where you can protect your retirement funds with creativity and flexibility. I encourage you to take these ideas back to your planner and see how they fit into your personalized retirement plan.

I wrote *The Retirement Endgame* to give you more control. I want to arm you with more knowledge, which in turn gives you more understanding, which in turn gives you the financial wisdom you need to make the best decisions.

That's a winning combination ... whether you're affluent or not!

Chapter 6

Life Insurance: The Misconceptions and the Truth that Wall Street is Hiding from You

Before we talk about life insurance, let's review the **Four Pillars of a Worry-free Financial Plan as discussed in chapter 4:**

1) Guarantee the safety of your principal

2) Control and flexibility of your money

3) A crediting method for growth on your money based on participation in the stock market gains, but not the losses

4) A lock-in mechanism that secures the growth of your account value to prevent losses during a future downturn.

So far in this book, we've mostly talked about the use of fixed guaranteed annuities to secure your retirement future. Annuities are the darlings of the Four Pillars. And yet, if you work with Wall Street brokers or have a lot of money, I'll bet you've gotten an earful about why you don't want or need annuities, and why these vehicles aren't right for you.

I'm here to tell you...some of those reasons are valid. Annuities are great investment vehicles, *when you need income.*

When $500,000 is the last dime you have to your name and you're laid off at fifty-five years old, income is exactly what you need. Or maybe you've got $1 million at age sixty-five in your pension plan, and that's it, Charlie. You might have made $100,000 a year, but now you've got to figure out how to take that $1 million, not lose a penny of it, and make it last for the next twenty years. How are you going to maintain the same annual income you had when you retired? Mathematically, it's not happening. Especially not if you lose any principal along the way.

If you have $1 million in retirement funds and you're getting 5 percent annually, that means you'll get around $75,000 a year for twenty years. What happens if that money is subject to Wall Street risk? What if the value goes down by 50 percent like it has **TWICE** in the last ten years? How long will that money last you then?

The answer is: not very. That's why a fixed annuity that guarantees you a set income can be a very good idea.

Most wealthy people fall into a different category. A person who's got $10 million doesn't need income; they need to hang on to the $10 million. So they come to me and say, "Why do I want an annuity? First of all, I don't need income. And second, my accountant told me I want to stay in stocks and bonds and real estate, because then when I die, my heirs will get the money with the stepped-up basis." (The stepped-up basis means that all of the capital gains on those assets that were in stocks, bonds, mutual funds, securities, and real estate are eliminated and the present value to the heirs is stepped up at the person's death.)

In an annuity, the money has been tax-deferred during the growth stage. That means that my clients with annuities have made, on average, 6 to 8 percent over the last twenty years. While that money is growing, it might double every twelve years. And if you hold an annuity that has deferred growth in it, that becomes ordinary income to the heirs. We might be talking $100,000 or $1 million, but regardless, that's not a good deal. Ordinary income is taxed as high as 42 percent, state and federal. This is why financial planners to the affluent often do not recommend annuities to their clients—because their heirs will pay a formidable price for that money.

While annuities can be fantastic vehicles for qualified retirement plans (because you're not going to spend that money; it's meant for income), they may not be the best place for your nonqualified funds. Non-qualified funds, remember, include all the money that is not in those qualified plans (IRA, TSP, 401k, etc.). It's the post-taxed money that's in the bank, the stock market, CDs, treasuries—wherever it is. So why would you want to put that liquid money into something that's going to have a non-stepped-up situation, leaving your estate vulnerable to getting clobbered with taxes?

This is the question foremost on the minds of my affluent clients. They want to know: If annuities aren't going to cut it, have you got something else for me?

As a matter of fact, I do.

Strategy #1:

Single-Pay Life Insurance – Its time has come!

My clients have been using this strategy for years, to great success. In many ways, a single-pay life insurance policy acts like an annuity: it grows tax-deferred. But here's what happens that makes it different.

Most of the time my clients don't touch their single-pay life insurance policies because they don't need income; they have other money. Unlike an annuity, these policies enable them to leverage a tax-free death benefit. This benefit goes to their estate or to their heirs, eliminating the objection that the money gets taxed heavily when they pass on. In fact it's even *better* than a stepped-up basis.

It's a stepped-up basis **plus additional money in tax-free life insurance** that you don't have with stocks and bonds.

More importantly, stocks and bonds don't give you any protection of principal. A single-pay **Index Universal Life** insurance program, on the other hand, is flexible, while giving you guaranteed principle, stock market growth without stock market risk, and a locked-in mechanism. Go ahead and check off every one of those Four Pillars with a check plus!

Another feature of the single-pay Index Universal Life insurance is your participation of the stock market growth the internal interest credits are about 2.5 times higher than what an annuity pays, meaning the caps are higher on how much you can make. Currently, you can participate in a single-pay life insurance policy and receive an annual return of caps of the S&P index, the Dow, the NASDAQ, the London Exchange—whatever index you want to track and participate in. Your money is not at risk; you're just getting a participation of the growth without the risk.

Most single-pay life insurance policies capture as high as 12-15 percent of that stock index return in that year. If the market did 25, you can make 12-15. If it did 10, you get all of the 10. If it did 20, you might get 12-15 of the 20 ... at no risk to you.

Compare this to most annuities, where you're looking at getting around 6-7 percent. Why? Because most people are not going to keep their money in annuities as long as they would in life insurance. They'll typically tap it for income. The insurance companies don't have the money long enough to make money on your money, so they can't pay you as high a participation rate. With life insurance, it's a longer hold for the insurance companies, so you get to participate with them in the process.

Simply put, they stand to gain more from your money, so they're willing to give you a bigger share of the winnings. In summary, a single-pay life insurance policy gives you the gift of accumulation. Like an annuity, you have no risk of principle, and you get a higher participation of stock index. You have as much flexibility, if not more, and you don't lose the stepped-up basis that you get with your stocks and bonds.

You now have a tax-free benefit that can be as much as 50 percent higher than what you've actually got in the cash value.

Now that's a pretty good deal for your heirs! Sorry, Wall Street. You want to object that life insurance can't be a good vehicle for creating and maintaining wealth? **Objection overruled.**

Strategy #2:

Creating Wealth for ages 30-50 Using Life Insurance to Create a Tax-Free Retirement

Did I get your attention with **tax-free retirement**?

I should hope so!

I stated in an earlier chapter why I recommend the use of a properly structured Universal Index Life policy to fund your retirement, but it bears repeating.

You want to accumulate tax-free, borrow out income tax-free, and have a leveraged higher cash benefit for your family tax-free.

If you are under age 50 and currently contributing to an unmatched 401(k) or IRA, you need to have your financial advisor do a long term comparison of between funding your retirement with stocks or mutual funds (uncertainty of performance and risk) to a Universal Index Life Policy. You'll be more than shocked at how well the life insurance measures up and surpasses the Wall Street Casino method of retirement planning.

The truth is that it's impossible to know where we'll be in five or ten or twenty years when it comes to taxes. Current tax laws are certainly in flux, and who knows where the estate tax, estate planning tax, or the income tax will end up? One thing we know for darn sure: they're not going to be lower. You don't solve the problem of a $16 trillion deficit by lowering the revenues that the country takes in. We're going to have to pay the piper for a lot of stupid decisions the government has made over the last twenty-five years. I'm not pointing fingers across party lines—I mean Democrats and Republicans alike.

If tax laws are going to be higher down the road—and believe me, they will be—you want to take advantage of anything that's going to give you tax-free income.

Currently, you get tax-free income from things like a Roth IRA. A Roth IRA is a nice vehicle, but in order to get one, you have to take your money out of your existing normal IRA, get taxed on it, and then convert it over so that the growth from that point forward will come out tax-free. Here's where the danger lies: they can change the rules at any time. I call it "**future tax-law risk**."

They might decide, for example, that it will no longer be fifty-nine and a half when you can access your

Roth. Maybe now you'll have to wait until you're sixty-five. Can they do that? Sure they can. They can also limit how much you're allowed to put into it. If you're under fifty, you can only put in $5,000 a year. If you're over fifty, you can put in $6,000 a year. What if you've got more than that? Tough luck—you've been restricted.

This is why I advise people to use life insurance to create a tax-free retirement. How?

By taking a lump sum of money that's not in your qualified plan, and repositioning that money into an **Index Universal Life Insurance** policy with a series of annual deposits. If you're under fifty, you do it with four annual deposits. If you're over fifty, you do it with five.

Let's say you have $1 million. If you're forty-eight, you put $250,000 into this type of policy each year, for the next four years. The reason you're doing this is that the IRS is requiring you to do it in order to create a tax-free loan provision. Down the road, you can withdraw the accumulation on that money, tax-free.

Plus you'll now have created a higher benefit than the cash value—income tax free—to your heirs.

Remember: you're doing this for your income—the income tax-free death benefit is just "gravy on the taters"!

Maybe you have $5-10,000,000 to your name, and you want to start earmarking some of that money for future income needs. This is the money you've identified **that you don't want to lose**. You need it down the road, in case things don't work out in your business ventures. This is not the money you get to play with; this is serious money. This goes in the "I can't afford to not have this in my future" pot.

We talked about the power of indexing in an earlier chapter, and how it exercises the **Four Pillars of *a Worry-free Financial Plan***. This same principle is true when it comes to life insurance. The crediting of the cash is using the same strategy. The good news about this vehicle is that you can access the money anytime. It's not a retirement plan; you don't have to wait until you're a certain age like you do with qualified plans or annuities. The downside to those vehicles is that you get taxed on the money that comes out before you reach a certain age. Because the life insurance policy is a tax-free loan, there are no restrictions. No tax. No age requirement. No strings attached.

You may be asking yourself, "What if they change the tax laws regarding tax-free loans in ten or fifteen years?" Great question— I'm glad you asked.

There's a rule in the US Constitution that has to do with contractual law called the **Ex Post Facto** provision. That's Latin for **"nothing after the fact."** Never in the history of our country has Congress come along and changed an existing constitutional provision that would affect past business contracts.

Instead, they say, "Everything up to this point is grandfathered under past law. From this point forward, it changes." What that means for you: if you've already established a life insurance contract, then you're grandfathered in.

I'm not saying they won't change it or can't change it. I'm saying it's not very likely because of that **Ex Post Facto** rule.

Another reason I like to use life insurance is that it makes great emergency money. If the last five years have taught us anything, it's to be prepared. I don't care how much money you've got: life happens. If you're breathing air, you're probably subject to some financial stress and uncertainty. Maybe your grandkids can no longer afford to go to college, because your kids lost their money in the stock market. Here you are, retired, with this money. How great would it be to go into a tax-free loan to help fund your grandkids' education?

I call that "family banking." Family banking gives you the opportunity to use your money to help your family, rather than having your money under the control of the bank or buried in real estate.

Remember what I've been saying throughout this book: if you're truly going to have a safe money plan, *you* have to be the one in control, not anybody else. With tax rates most likely on the rise, a tax-free strategy is the right strategy to have.

Strategy #3:

Tax-Deductible Life Insurance

"What?" you're saying. "**Tax-deductible dollars**? I was told I couldn't buy life insurance inside a qualified plan!"

The secret to this strategy—buying life insurance with tax-deductible dollars you already have in your plan—is in the source of how the premium payments are made.

Let's review how it works. We'll say you have a 401(k) with $1 million in it. You've just turned fifty-nine and a half (happy half birthday), so you are able to do a transfer into your IRA called an "**in-service, non-hardship distribution**" (more on that in the next chapter). Ninety-five percent of the plans out there, including government-deferred compensation plans, can be transferred into an IRA or another qualified plan vehicle (Solo 401(k), Self-Employed IRA or SEP, TSP, etc.). We talked about this in a prior chapter — how to continue to work at your job while moving your money to a place where *you* control the investment of your assets, rather than leaving it in a 401(k) where you have minimal control. The IRS is not concerned because it's only a temporary tax-free transfer; but they're going to get their pound of flesh a little later down the road.

Here's what you can do in a solo 401(k) that you can't do in an IRA or a 401(k). **You can take 25 percent of your assets and purchase a life insurance policy with it.** So you have $1 million and you do an *in-service* *distribution*, or you've retired. You take that 401(k) and move it to a solo 401(k). Most of you who have that kind of money aren't really retiring; you're still doing some sort of consulting work. So you take out $250,000, and you put the remaining $750,000 into a fixed index annuity that's going to begin to get interest crediting and grow.

You'll probably get a guarantee on that account, and you'll use that for income down the road as needed.

With the $250,000, you're going to buy a single-pay life insurance policy. As I explained in **Strategy #1**, you're going to be able to buy a leveraged amount of death benefit ("leveraged" meaning **more** than what you put into it). So if you put $250,000 into a life insurance policy, you'll more than likely get $500,000+ of death benefits, income tax-free. The $250,000 is the cash value part of it, but if you die, there's an extra amount of money that will be created.

What happens is that, in this case, you've used tax-deductible dollars. You don't pay any additional premiums, and you're sitting there with a life insurance policy that at your death will pay out probably two or three times what you put into it. **That's tax-free money to your**

beneficiaries! All you have to put back into the solo 401(k) is the original $250,000 premium you started with.

Everything else gets to stay with the estate — income tax-free!

Strategy #4:

Funding Your Retirement by Buying a Life Policy on One of Your Parents

I have a client, let's call him Joe who is forty-four years old and his mom was sixty-three. I bought a life insurance policy for several hundred thousand dollars on his mom's life. For the last fifteen years, he paid for that policy. **It hasn't cost her a cent**.

Why did I recommend that? I figured out that between age sixty-three and eight-five (which was his mother's life expectancy), he would pay about $80,000 into that policy. And while there's no way to know for certain which of them will pass on to the other side of the curtain first, more than likely, his mother will go before he will. When she passes, he will get a tax-free benefit of over $300,000 for his family. That's a tax-free benefit!

The $80,000 he spent along the way is part of his retirement plan. At forty-four, he knew that he'd be working for the next twenty-five years. He sat down with my mom and said, "How would you like to make sure that I have some money for my retirement without costing you a dime? And I promise not to kill you!"

She laughed and said, "Of course!" It was an easy way for her to help enhance the retirement planning for his family, without using any of her retirement savings.

The wealthiest parents in the world already have life insurance policies. The Gates and the Rockefellers— they're already using these strategies. They've had life insurance policies their whole lives. Many parents don't, and it's a great way to bolster **your** retirement plan without costing **them** any additional money. Parents are usually fine with it ... as long as they trust you not to knock 'em off!

I'm half joking, of course, but in all seriousness, the trust factor is important. Before you broach this idea with your parents, make sure they know that you genuinely have their best interest and well-being at heart.

You can use the insurability of your parents to fund your retirement, or set up a college fund for your children, and their grandchildren. It may seem like a hefty investment, but when you look at what it costs to buy the life insurance, compared to the tax-free benefits, you'll see why it's worth it.

Joe will get over $300,000 of income tax-free death benefits that's equal to about $550,000 — if it were in his fully-taxable IRA. In order to make this same return on Wall Street, he'd have to be guaranteed 15 percent a year. Good luck getting 10 percent consistently with Wall Street!

So you now have some ways to make the most of the dollars in your non-Qualified savings using life insurance.

Chapter 7

The Truth about Home Equity Management

Is having a house free and clear of debt the best way to go?

Not necessarily. And here's why.

In his best-selling book *Missed Fortune 101*, retirement strategist Douglas Andrew states: "The most important elements of home equity management are maintaining liquidity and safety of principal and creating the opportunity for home equity to grow in a separate side fund, where it is accessible in the event of an emergency."

For example, a couple comes into my office and asks me to give them counsel on the largest investment of their lifetime. They say to me, "Help us retire securely. What kind of an investment should we make?" Then I give them some features of an investment that they might consider as follows: 1) you can determine the amount of money you put into it; 2) you can set up a schedule of future investment contributions; 3) you can contribute more each month than what's originally scheduled; 4) all the money you put into the investment, however, is not liquid and not safe from loss; 5) this investment earns no returns; 6) your income tax liability will increase with each contribution; and 7) finally, when this investment plan is complete, it would not pay you a dime of income for your retirement. Now I ask them, "Sound good to you?"

"Of course not," says the husband, "who in the heck would make such an investment? There is no liquidity, flexibility, rate of return, or tax advantages. It's against the four pillars of financial planning you talked about."

Then the wife tugs the husband's sleeve and says to him, "**Honey, doesn't that kind of sound like our mortgage?**"

The truth is that the mortgage does more good than you know. Not only does it help you finance your home, but it helps finance your retirement. I'm going to show you how the mortgage is actually your friend.

The Arbitrage System

The prevalent myth nowadays says there are two kinds of people in the world: those who earn interest and those who pay interest. People who earn interest go to the bank, put $100,000 in a CD, and get 2 percent returns on their money. Others pay interest on the loans they take out to start a business or to buy a house.

I say there is a third person out there who both pays and earns interest.

Like the big banks, this third person understands the power of using other people's money. In the banks' case, they make money with your money. For instance, you go to a local bank, put $100,000 on a CD, and get a 2 percent return for the next year. You think the bank's just going to put your $100,000 in a vault? It's just paying you 2 percent because they feel good about having extra money in the vault? No! They will loan the money at a 5 to 8 percent interest rate to someone who is buying a house or a car or 10-30 percent to someone who is paying for things by credit card and so on. Overtime, the bank desires to make at least 2-3 percent annually on your money. That doesn't sound like much but think about all the people who would give $100,000 to the bank. Their contributions add up to billions of dollars of deposits for the bank. The bank makes a profit by loaning out the billions. This system is called "arbitrage."

Arbitrage is a system that gives you profit based on the difference between what you pay in interest and what you earn in interest. With arbitrage, you borrow on one rate and invest in another rate. In addition to banks, insurance companies also follow this system when they sell you annuities. That is why banks and insurance companies are among the wealthiest institutions in the world. (I'm talking about financially prudent banks …. not the small banks that have failed in the recent economy for making bad loans.)

Having a mortgage also allows you to take advantage of the arbitrage system. You can take out a mortgage with an interest rate of 5 percent and invest the money that you otherwise would have put into the house into a safe savings strategy to collect returns of 7 percent. In the end, you will collect positive returns from your investments from borrowing at a net after-tax 3 percent and receiving 5 percent after tax considerations. If you pay cash for the house in the beginning, you will not be able to collect this kind of arbitrage.

The Importance of Liquidity

Nothing beats having cash on hand during gloomy economic times. If you lose your job, get divorced, or get sick, it will really suck that you don't have liquid assets. You would be forced to liquidate assets like your house or car—you would have to sell them for cash at fire-sale prices. On the other hand, people who have cash liquidity can slide by emergencies, meet their expenses, and do grocery shopping, unlike the people without liquid assets. Taking out a mortgage and not trying to repay it as fast as you can will give you emergency cash by separating it from your house or removing it from your backyard as I like to say.

How Safe Is Your Home Equity?

Home equity is defined as the difference between the market value of the house and the value of the loan (market value minus loan value). If the value of your house is $500,000 and you have $400,000 in mortgages, your home equity is $100,000.

If you have a house paid free and clear, and you experience a flat real estate market for 10 years, your home equity would stay the same without gains or losses. However, if you experience a market loss of 30-50 percent (and these numbers are based on reality), then your home equity would be significantly reduced. You just saw the largest asset you own depreciate. Therefore, it's not safe to put all your money in the house. Home equity is not safe from market decline.

What's the Rate of Return on Your Home Equity?

If you bought a house in 2005 for $500,000, and it is worth $250,000 today, you not only got a zero rate of return, but you experienced a 50 percent loss. The traditional real estate market experiences a 20 to 30 percent loss every 10-12 years or so. It's all a game of supply and demand; when the demand decreases, the prices fall. Easy lending practices create a hot real estate market, but it takes about ten years to make up a 30 percent loss. The value of your house will have to grow 43 percent in order to get back to its purchasing price. And it's not easy to climb back through a depressed real estate market. We're not even sure how long it will take to flush out the bad loans and the extra supply for homes (due to the lack of ability to buy) in the recent market. It's been several years, and experts think some markets may take several more years to get back to 2007 levels of home values.

From my analysis of over sixty years of historical data on real estate cycles, it usually takes about six to eight years to get from the bottom of the real estate market to its peak. When can you expect to regain your losses from those down years? The math is simple: Your house was valued at $500,000 in 2005. In 2009, it is valued at $350,000. In 2015, hopefully but not likely, the value may come back to $500,000. And how much did you make during those 10 years? The answer is zero.

What about Reverse Mortgages to assist your Retirement Plans for income?

Let's say, optimistically, that you have $1 million in your 401(k). If you take money out of it, it's fully taxable. You might be sixty-five years old and plan to take $75,000 out annually for the rest of your life.   If it's not in the guaranteed safe money plan, who's to say that million dollars won't turn into $500,000 overnight? It's the ole primary need of the return **of** your money not just return **on** your money.

Let me ask you a question: In light of all the trillions of dollars thrown overboard to rescue the passengers of the sinking ship "**USS Wall Street**," do you think income and estate taxes will go UP, DOWN, or STAY THE SAME over the next five to ten years? If you are a company that needs to increase cash flow to survive, and all things being equal, do you need to lower revenues or increase revenues? There's your answer as to where taxes are heading.

So let's say you've done a pretty good job at saving, and you have a good pension from the state, government, or company; plus you have social security and income off other investments. What happens if you are taxed 50 percent when taxes increase instead of your current 30 percent? Then you would only less income to spend— your lifestyle will be greatly affected. The point is that the 401(k) is not reliable, as it is an IRS lien on your retirement future, and you don't know the particulars of the lien as the rules can and will change over the next twenty years (how it's taxed, when it's available without penalty, and other yet-to-be-disclosed tax law changes on the horizon). This is the danger of having only a 401K or other fully taxable pension plan as your primary source of income and a paid up home where the equity provides no additional income to you as taxes and inflation tears into your retirement lifestyle.

I'm a big advocate of **reverse mortgages** for those people who have all their retirement strategy tied up in their qualified plans and home equity, and who face a possible reduction of their lifestyles when (not if) taxes increase. And maybe they have lost a significant portion of their nest egg over the past several years. I suggest to people who are over sixty-eight years old and who have at least 50 percent equity in their properties to look at **reverse mortgages** to provide a significant increase in their retirement incomes to make up for reductions from taxes, market losses, and potential medical expenses.

The only limitation this couple qualifying for the reverse mortgage is that the youngest spouse has to be sixty-three or older. All you have to do is to call your bank and ask for a reverse mortgage on your house. Such a move requires no qualifying, or out-of-pocket expenses, other than paying for the appraisal; all you need is to keep your property taxes, property insurance and association fees current. Note that your family or the state has 6-12 months after your death to either sell the house to repay the loan you took out or refinance the house and keep it.

Here's an example where a reverse mortgage would make sense. A retired couple (age seventy-five) has a home valued at $750,000 in 2006 with a $200,000 mortgage with a $2200 monthly payment—and not much liquidity other than a diminished 401K account after Wall Street got done with them. By October 2011, the home dropped in value to $450,000, and the retired owner still has a $200,000 in mortgage.

This retired couple should look at a reverse mortgage for about $350,000 to pay off that $200,000 mortgage (and save the $2200 monthly payment) and keep $150,000. I would put $50,000 into the bank for safety and liquidity, and create additional income over the next ten years for $1000 monthly with the $100,000 in a safe money strategy. **That's a $3200 per month positive swing in their favor!**

What about the children and the estate, you might ask? Well, I say to those kids that unless they are willing to write a $2000 monthly check to Mom and Dad's retirement for the rest of their lives, **stop complaining**.

For every person who doesn't understand the importance of safety, liquidity, and rate of return on your real estate equity, I have found three who get it. If you don't feel comfortable following my advice, yet you believe in the math, please tell your friends and family to call me. Helping others with their retirement planning is part of the good-old sowing and reaping life philosophy.

A Final Word on Real Estate Investing

Real estate entails risk. So when you do buy additional real estate, do so according to your budget. Put as little down as possible and keep your money liquid on a side pot to cover unforeseen emergencies, repairs, and cash flow needs. Never put every dime you have into another investment property, the stock market, or a limited partnership that entails risk you can't afford. You must have liquidity so that you are able to handle potential financial emergencies caused by a lack of control of your money.

Chapter 8

The Retirement Endgame Process

Now that you've seen all the problems that traditional, high-risk Wall Street-style investing entails, you may be asking, "How do I get started on moving my money to safer ground? And who can help me do that?" As someone who has shown you what a brighter day can look like for your retirement, I'm not going to leave you standing in the rain.

The retirement planning industry uses two ways to find clients: the "hard sell" process and the "buy when ready" process.

Wall Street only uses the **"hard sell"** process. Here's how it works:

Step 1)

Without a clue about your retirement options, you walk into an asset management firm—we could call it Schwab or Fidelity, but we could just as easily call it

Gambling With Your Money, Inc. You are relying on someone to guide you in the right direction. You figure that since these people are wearing nice suits and working out of nice offices, they must know what they're talking about when it comes to securing your financial future.

Of course, they don't, but that doesn't stop them from saying, or their prospects from believing, what they're told from the knucklehead managers on the higher floors.

Step 2)

Upon the advice of an advisor at Gambling With Your Money, Inc., you invest in stocks, or stock/bond mutual funds. It doesn't matter what kind of person you are, whether you're rich or middle class or old, young, or somewhere in the middle. As long as you have the money to invest, Wall Street advisors will sell you the same products. Those products are usually stock mutual funds and bond funds. Why? If you've read this far into the book, you know the answer: **Those "investments" make the investment bookies and their casinos the most money.**

The "**hard sell**" process takes place anytime Wall Street can take advantage of your lack of knowledge, understanding, or control. It's like walking into a Best Buy without knowing what kind of TV you want to buy, and suddenly the salesman is in your face with a deal for anything from a small HD TV to a complete $10,000 home entertainment system! The salesperson might end up trying to sell the high-end stuff when your needs and budget don't call for that product. It's not the salesman's fault that you walked into the store completely unprepared and uneducated concerning your needs.

Can you see the similarity in how most people buy their investments that will supposedly secure their financial futures?

In the "**hard sell**" process at Gambling With Your Money, Inc. and other Wall Street casinos, buyers make decisions based on emotion rather than on information that they understand and that fits into their pre-determined needs and boundaries. (And even though they think they understand the information given by the bookie, what happens when what they are given is misinformation?)

How many people do you see at the mall buying supplemental nutritional pills because of mass marketing in health magazines and TV infomercials or on the advice of their "health advisor," Dr. Neighbor? Do you think they've consulted their doctors or health care professionals about what their actual nutritional deficiencies are?

Likewise, we all know a person who got too excited about a refrigerator on the showroom floor of Best Buy and bought it on emotion only to realize that his new fridge doesn't fit into the designated spot in the kitchen? He was overwhelmed by the sight of the ice dispenser and gauges on the appliance, the sales talk of the sales associate, and the 15 percent-off coupon he found online. What a deal! Unfortunately, he let his emotions get the best of him and forgot to do the basic research on what size refrigerator would actually fit in his house and what his needs were --- before he walked into the store!

Remember that the Wall Street salesperson has to create the fear in you that if you don't buy his product, then you might miss the boat on the Casino's action. Even if you suggest to him that you are not interested in risking money you can't afford to lose, he will still try to convince you that you are wrong and that you really need this investment in order to secure your retirement future. You know: no risk, no reward!

That's the "**hard sell**" process. They're coming at you unsolicited by phone, dinner workshop invitations, or direct mail advertising to sell you stock and bond funds...but they're really selling you out because you have no game plan to deal with the onslaught of information that you're not sure will work for you.

The good news is that Coach Jerry Whitmire has a new game plan for you!

Using **The Retirement Endgame**, you'll discover that I've created a system that uses a "**buy when ready**" process. "**Buy when ready**" means that you are doing things with a plan versus no plan at all.

When you come into our "store," you'll already have a plan based on your core values, the things that make you happy and content, and your investment parameters. Your plan objective will most certainly be to keep your money safe while growing your investments for retirement. If you didn't have this plan, you wouldn't have come to us in the first place. You'd be like those people standing outside Gambling With Your Money, Inc. or one of its many competitor casinos, waiting for the doors to open and waving your checkbook at the first bookie you see.

That's not you.

The problem that exists in the Wall Street "**hard sell**" process is that most people don't possess the knowledge, time, and financial aptitude to discern what investment option lines up with their parameters of knowledge, understanding, and control. People need the opportunity to educate themselves at their own paces about their financial goals, rather than having a stranger tell them what they need or do not need before they're fully ready to make an important decision.

Our process begins with a familiarization process acquired through this book, our website videos and content, or our **Retirement Endgame** educational workshops. In this way, you gain the information on the strategies and products available to help you decide if our system complements the pre-determined life goals for you and your family.

Four Step Process for Successful Relationship Building

So how do the relationships between us and our client differ from what goes on in the Wall Street Casino? I'm glad you asked! I have four strategies for Client Relationship Management that made the success stories that you just read possible.

They are: **Education, Evaluation, Implementation, and Preservation.**

Let's first discuss **Education**. My clients found me; I didn't hunt them down. They attended an educational workshop, visited our website, read about me in an interview in the media, heard me on the radio, or were referred to me by satisfied clients. **The Retirement Endgame** and the fundamental beliefs of our company resonated in their hearts. So in the first stage of my relationship with my client, I educate them about safe investments and about the system of risk on Wall Street.

The second stage is the **Evaluation** of the client's investment goals, parameters, and their lives in a broader sense. I want to help people discover a personalized strategy for their money that fits in with their goals and values. For example, a father makes $200,000 a year and is highly taxed. He has to figure out how to put four kids through college in the future, including giving them the option of going to private colleges. How is he going to do that without compromising his retirement future? How do his kids' educational expenses fit in the picture with his retirement security?

With **The Retirement Endgame**, it's very important for us to develop a retirement plan that incorporates all the pieces of a client's life.

Retirement planning is similar to the art of interior design. The designer has to make the wallpaper of the home fit with the furniture and overall decor of the house. If the owners of the home are a conservative couple that listens to opera all the time, the designer shouldn't recommend polka-dot wallpaper that clashes with their dark-hued sofas, right?

In order to make my investment recommendations fit in with the lifestyles and dreams of my clients, I ask them during the initial evaluation: "Pretend it is three years from now; what do you want to see happen with your finances, career, and personal life that would make you feel good about your progress in those areas?" This question gets them thinking about their goals and values and not about the products I can offer them. In turn, their answers give me a better idea of their parameters and dreams, so that I may recommend to them the right financial products for their retirement. Remember how we talked about how important it is for people to know their limits? It's just as important for their financial advisor to know his clients' limits. Otherwise, how can he create the right plan for them?

The third stage is **Implementation** or execution of my safe money plan. I prepare the plan and revise it as desired by my client. Then, I put it into place.

Finally, the fourth stage is the **Preservation** of our client relationships. **The Retirement Endgame** is constantly developing ways to give our clients up-to-date information about the financial environment, including regular educational emails and videos on our website (**www.theretirementendgame.com**) that I update regularly to keep my clients informed.

Lack of focus is the surest way to kill the planning that will achieve your dreams.

It is of paramount importance that my clients are educated and reminded of their desire to stay the course in their safe money solutions, so that they aren't tempted to return to the Wall Street casino when people around them start bragging about how much they won at the "tables." I need to constantly remind them of what happened in 2007-2009, 2000-2003, 1991-1994, 1987, 1982, and even back in the early 1970s. At this writing, world stock markets are once again in chaos after a six year recovery born out of lax Fed policy and easy money to Wall Street Banks, and a steady diet of increasing debt.

I could be writing this book in 10 years, and one thing is sure: the markets will be up ---- or down. The fact is, you can't afford to gamble with money you can't afford to lose.

Client relationships are very important to me, and I want to make sure that my advice is available to them whenever they need it. People need to be reminded that gambling is an attitude that permeates American society. Betting is everywhere: sports, investments, and even odds on who is voted off reality TV shows! If that's your idea of entertainment, fine, but don't let it cross over into the way you think about managing your money!

So what's it going to be? Will you call up a brokerage house like Gambling With Your Money, Inc. for the "hard sell" process, or will you visit our office for the **"buy when ready"** process?

Chapter 9

Some Final Thoughts

By now, you know me pretty well. You know what I believe about investing. You know how I feel about risk in general and about the way the Wall Street casino peddles risk, taking advantage of investors' fear (and greed) and their desire to look good and sound cool at cocktail parties. You know how I feel about the importance of sleeping soundly at night because your money, retirement, and future are safe. You know my spiritual core and my thoughts about how money fits into a balanced life. You even know that I take my own advice.

Although we've never met, I know a lot about you—simply because you've read this book all the way to the end. I know that you're a hard-working person who takes your responsibilities in life seriously—at work, at home, and in your financial life. I know that either you or people you know well have been burned by Wall Street and that over the years you've witnessed tens, or even hundreds, of thousands of hard-earned dollars vanish once the music stopped. I know you've always believed there was a better way. I'd like to believe you've found it now.

Many people may never invest with me, and I understand that fact. You can't be all things to all people. As we've discussed, I'll never attract the get-rich-quick types, the people who go from infomercial to seminar, waving their credit cards at the "gurus" who may not know how to enrich you, but they sure know how to enrich themselves. The penny stock pickers, the day traders, the people who think they'll make a fortune trading stock options or buying and flipping foreclosures (at the same time that people who actually know something about real estate are going bust) ... they're not in my sights, and I'm not in theirs.

However, you're different.

You're too smart to fall for the hype. I've deliberately written this book in a straightforward, down-to-earth, easy-to-understand manner because the concepts I've sought to share with you in these pages are exactly that: straightforward, down to earth, and easy to understand.

Risk is bad.

- A loss is more dangerous to your overall financial health than a gain benefits you.

- If you don't have understanding, knowledge, and control over your money, than someone else does. And he's more likely to make profits himself than help you.

- **The market doesn't just go up**. It goes down, and when it goes down, it takes the hard-earned money of many good people with it. The brokers live to sell another day, but you don't have another twenty years to make up for the money you can lose in a matter of months.

- As an investment philosophy, **discernment beats fear and greed every time**. It was true in King Solomon's day, and it's equally true in ours.

- If you can't explain an investment to your twelve-year-old, then you shouldn't be making that investment.

- Wall Street's system is for accumulating money ... and it fails desperately at preserving and distributing it to the people who need it.

After the Great Depression of 2008-2011, when it came time to take responsibility for the loss of trillions of dollars of investor wealth, Wall Street blamed everyone but itself. "Trust us," they said. However, when the market collapsed, Wall Street's tune changed. It became, "You should never have trusted us."

For all the illegal activity and deliberate misinformation from the banking and mortgage industry and the Wall Street Casino that was laid upon the folks who couldn't afford to lose money, **NO ONE WENT TO JAIL.**

You're probably thinking, "If this stuff is so obvious, why doesn't everybody preach it?"

By now, you know the answer. There's more money for Wall Street in keeping the status quo of tapping into people's fear and greed, so they can tap into their pocketbooks. A commission here, a fee there...it all adds up to money out of your account and into their pockets. Where do you think they get the money to pay themselves those obscene salaries and bonuses ... from thin air?

No, from hard-working people like you!

I'm sure you realize just how passionate I am about working with people like you to protect your investment and keep it safe, so that you can count on the money now and in the future.

I hope this book has been a blessing in solving your need for a safe retirement future, without Wall Street risk.

Your intention to have your assets protected needs your action to do so.

If you would like to discuss how these safe money strategies can protect your financial future, please call or email me to set up a short conference call or meeting at my office.

Jerry Whitmire

jerry@theretirementendgame.com

Phone: (480) 620-6777

Visit us at:

www.theretirementendgame.com